Butterflies

Pollinators and Nectar-Sippers

by Adele D. Richardson

Consultant:
Eileen McDonnell, President
Southeastern Pennsylvania Chapter
North American Butterfly Association

Bridgestone Books
an imprint of Capstone Press
Mankato, Minnesota

Bridgestone Books are published by Capstone Press
151 Good Counsel Drive, P.O. Box 669, Mankato, Minnesota 56002
http://www.capstone-press.com

Library of Congress Cataloging-in-Publication Data
Richardson, Adele, 1966–
    Butterflies: pollinators and nectar-sippers/by Adele D. Richardson.
        p. cm.—(The wild world of animals)
    Includes bibliographical references and index.
    ISBN 0-7368-0824-8
    1. Butterflies—Juvenile literature. [1. Butterflies.] I. Title. II. Series.
QL544.2 .R53 2001
595.78'9—dc21

                                                                        00-010180

Summary: A simple introduction to butterflies describing their physical characteristics,
habitat, young, food, enemies, and relationship to people.

Editorial Credits
Sarah Lynn Schuette, editor; Karen Risch, product planning editor; Linda Clavel,
    designer and illustrator; Kimberly Danger and Heidi Schoof, photo researchers

Photo Credits
Connie Toops, 14
GeoIMAGERY/Fred Siskind, cover, 10; Mildred Ladyman, 4; Bev Murphy, 12;
    Jan W. Jorolan, 16
PhotoDisc, Inc., 1
Rob and Ann Simpson, 8, 18, 20
Visuals Unlimited/Richard Norman, 6

Table of Contents

pink-spotted cattleheart

antennas

proboscis

wings

Butterflies

Butterflies have six thin legs and four wings. They have two large eyes and two long antennas. Butterflies have a mouth called a proboscis. The proboscis is shaped like a tube.

antenna
a feeler on the head of an insect

blue buckeye

head

thorax

abdomen

Butterflies Are Insects

Butterflies are insects. Insects have an outer shell instead of a skeleton. Most insects also have six legs and two antennas. Insect bodies have three parts. They have a head, a thorax, and an abdomen.

abdomen
a stomach

clear-tipped swallowtail

FUN FACTS

Between 12,000 and 15,000 kinds of butterflies live in the world. They do not live in Antarctica. The temperature in Antarctica is too cold for butterflies.

A World of Butterflies

Butterflies live in gardens, forests, grasslands, and many other habitats around the world. Butterflies often sun themselves on trees and flowers. They need to be warm to fly. Some butterflies migrate to warmer places during winter.

migrate
to move from one place to another

monarch caterpillar hatching

Butterfly Eggs

Butterflies mate during spring and summer. Females lay eggs on plants a few hours after mating. Some female butterflies lay one egg. Others lay up to 1,500 eggs. Butterfly eggs usually hatch in a few days. Some butterfly eggs take months to hatch.

mate
to join together to produce young

anise swallowtail caterpillar

Caterpillars

Caterpillars hatch from butterfly eggs. They have large jaws and many legs. Caterpillars often eat green plants and grow very fast. Caterpillars then molt and crawl out of their old skin.

molt
to shed skin so that
new skin can grow

monarch

Changing into an Adult

A caterpillar changes into a hard shell called a chrysalis. An adult butterfly grows inside the chrysalis. The adult has wet wings when it breaks out of the chrysalis. The new butterfly has to dry its wings before it can fly away.

eastern tiger swallowtail

Nectar-Sippers

Butterflies are nectar-sippers. They do not have any teeth or jaws. A butterfly uses its proboscis to sip nectar from the inside of flowers. The proboscis is like a straw.

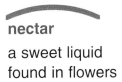

nectar
a sweet liquid
found in flowers

olive juniper hairstreak

FUN FACTS

Some butterflies are poisonous to the animals that eat them. Other butterflies give off bad smells to scare animals away.

Hiding from Enemies

Butterflies have many enemies. Birds, frogs, and spiders eat butterflies and caterpillars. Many butterflies have wings that look like leaves or flowers. These butterflies use their camouflage to hide from enemies. They sit still and blend into their habitat.

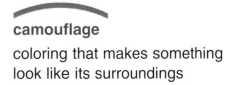

camouflage
coloring that makes something look like its surroundings

ruby lacewing

Pollinators

Butterflies help plants and flowers grow by carrying pollen from one flower to another. Plants need pollen to grow. Some people plant butterfly gardens with flowers that butterflies pollinate. These people enjoy watching the butterflies that live near their homes.

pollen
tiny yellow grains found inside flowers; plants need pollen to grow.

Hands On: Pollination

Butterflies help to grow new flowers and plants. Pollen from a flower or plant rubs off on a butterfly's legs and wings. Butterflies then carry the pollen to other flowers and plants. This process is called pollination.

What You Need:

Water
2 white tissues
Black pepper
2 cotton swabs

What You Do:

1. Wet each tissue with a few drops of water and crumple it up into a ball.
2. Sprinkle black pepper on one of the tissue balls.
3. Use the cotton swabs to pick up the peppered ball. Set it down and use the cotton swabs to pick up the other ball.

Pepper from the first ball rubs off onto the cotton swabs. The cotton swabs then leave pepper on the second ball. The black pepper is like pollen. The cotton swabs are like the butterfly's legs.

Words to Know

camouflage (KAM-uh-flahzh)—coloring that makes something look like its surroundings; butterflies use camouflage to hide from enemies.

caterpillar (KAT-ur-pil-ur)—the second life stage of a butterfly; caterpillars hatch from eggs.

chrysalis (KRISS-uh-liss)—the third life stage of a butterfly; a chrysalis is a hard shell where an adult butterfly forms.

habitat (HAB-uh-tat)—the place where an animal lives; butterflies live in gardens, forests, and grasslands.

migrate (MYE-grate)—to move from one place to another; butterflies migrate to warm places during winter.

proboscis (pro-BOS-kiss)—a tube that insects use to drink liquid; butterflies sip nectar through a proboscis.

Read More

Holmes, Kevin J. *Butterflies.* Animals. Mankato, Minn.: Bridgestone Books, 1998.

Schaffer, Donna. *Painted Lady Butterflies.* Life Cycles. Mankato, Minn.: Bridgestone Books, 1999.

Wallace, Karen. *Born to Be a Butterfly.* Dorling Kindersley Readers. New York: Dorling Kindersley, 2000.

Internet Sites

All About Butterflies
http://www.EnchantedLearning.com/subjects/butterfly

Butterflies, On the Wings of Freedom
http://library.thinkquest.org/27968/kids_intro.shtml

Children's Butterfly Site
http://www.mesc.usgs.gov/butterfly/butterfly.html

Index